The New Age Bedtime Stories

By Sue Ellen Rodrigues

Illustrated By Deepa Pawar

AF428500

Copyright © Sue Ellen Rodrigues
All Rights Reserved.

This book has been self-published with all reasonable efforts taken to make the material error-free by the author. No part of this book shall be used, reproduced in any manner whatsoever without written permission from the author, except in the case of brief quotations embodied in critical articles and reviews.

The Author of this book is solely responsible and liable for its content including but not limited to the views, representations, descriptions, statements, information, opinions and references ["Content"]. The Content of this book shall not constitute or be construed or deemed to reflect the opinion or expression of the Publisher or Editor. Neither the Publisher nor Editor endorse or approve the Content of this book or guarantee the reliability, accuracy or completeness of the Content published herein and do not make any representations or warranties of any kind, express or implied, including but not limited to the implied warranties of merchantability, fitness for a particular purpose. The Publisher and Editor shall not be liable whatsoever for any errors, omissions, whether such errors or omissions result from negligence, accident, or any other cause or claims for loss or damages of any kind, including without limitation, indirect or consequential loss or damage arising out of use, inability to use, or about the reliability, accuracy or sufficiency of the information contained in this book.

Made with ♥ on the Notion Press Platform
www.notionpress.com

Dedication:

The art of storytelling is a gift. Anyone can tell a story, but not everyone can bring it to life. My Dad, Mr. Gordon Rodrigues, AKA Tiger, had a unique quality of mastering this art. From a very young age, I remember Dad telling us stories to put us to bed, keep us quiet or just entertain us. It was NEVER the usual Jack and the Beanstalk, or Cinderella, or Snow White. It was stories narrated from his childhood - some real and most of them imaginary. He had not an iota of boring or dull energy in him. An English Teacher by profession and a Certified Toast Master and Trainer, his stories sparked eagerness, enthusiasm, and enigmatic energy that we were engaged and entralled right throughout. He made it vibrant, vivacious, and voracious. And now I know he'd be smirking down upon me loving the fact that I used alliterations to express this.

Dad's stories were a class apart. It ranged from funny to scary (ofcourse when we were older). Stories of a dog named Rover, of railway colony life, of mischievous flirting encounters, of climbing trees, scaling walls, bike expeditions, of big hand-driven fans that were operated manually by punkhawallas (a term used to describe attendants in India who manually operated these fans with a pulley system) and a big bed shared by 7 siblings, of wolves howling on traveling sprees, of a dead man playing the guitar under a tree, of many many twisted untold crazy incorrigible tales that probably no one could ever have imagined.

His self made quotes were outrageous yet unique. He had written many a school song and many literary pieces of art. He taught us not to procrastinate and always said "if you want something done well, do it yourself". He taught us to take our own decisions after a certain age by his famous quote "you make your bed, you lie on it". In jest he would say "dog also won't eat it", to pull our leg stating that the food made was horrible. To toughen us up he'd always say "God helps those who help themselves". He believed that music was the food of love, Shakespeare was a Guru, and knew almost any piece of literature, author, or poet in any century and language. He even kept himself updated with modern art, music, and literature. He taught us the art of camouflage, or of how not to make a "mountain out of a mole hill" and so much much more. If only we could paint a picture of his exuberant mind, it would probably speak a zillion different things. Never a dull moment. NEVER!

From his children to his grandchildren, nieces and nephews, grand nieces and grand nephews, every child who Dad came in contact with, has had an amazing adventure or experience to relate. He knew how to play chill and still thrill. Such was his love for kids. Such was his vibe. Such was his aura. And I am truly blessed to have attained a small, if not large piece of this gift from him - love for children & stories.

This book is dedicated to my Dad, my Hero, my Ultimate StoryTeller. He personally read and edited each and every story before his sad demise on February 3rd, 2025. He waited eagerly for this to be published but I guess destiny had other plans. Love and miss you terribly Dad and thank you for giving me as you said "Your Heart & Your Brains" - my 2 most prized possessions.

Love Always,
Your Small Dollar Girl

Sue Ellen Rodrigues

Book Acknowledgement

Thank you dear dad, Gordon Rodrigues, for being the literary genius I was always inspired by. My gift of writing is one I owe to you now and forever!

Thank you mom, Jennifer Rodrigues, for being my supporter in everything I do!

Thank you to my biggest fan, my best friend, Michelle Ann Danda, for always believing in me and my prose & poetry!

A BIG SHOUT OUT to my Illustrator and friend, Deepa Pawar, without whose help this would not have been possible.

Lastly, but not the least, thank you to my husband, Sanjay James, and special hugs to my children to whom this book is dedicated: Zoey Evan James and Zander Eben James.

Love to all!

Patience

Patience was a pretty five-year-old, quite adored by everyone.
Amelia and Patience were best friends.

One day Amelia was crying because her little brother had taken away her favourite toy – a broken bicycle.

Amelia tugged her mother's clothes while she was cooking asking for the bicycle. She yelled on top of her voice "mommieeeeeee.... I want that bicycle now, now now!"

Her mother explained to Amelia that little Tom would soon get bored with it and she can then have it back.
But Amelia kept crying.

Her father was a very hard working man. He said "Amelia darling could you please wait until your birthday next month?
We will save up some money and buy you a brand new bicycle."

But Amelia was impatient and screamed even louder "it's not fair, it's not fair"! That is my bicycle and I want it now!".

Just then Patience walked in. She spoke to Amelia gently and said "Amelia please be patient dear. Your father said he would buy you a new one for your birthday next month"

She hugged Amelia and also said "You do know that you won't get a toy back any sooner if you cry and scream. Also, little babies do get bored very quickly and turn to the next toy!"

Just as she said that, Tom turned away from the broken bicycle and went to play with another toy. It was right enough!

Amelia realized her mistake. She thanked Patience for teaching her this virtue. She remembered that everything had a place and time and "if she cried right now for something, it would definitely not get to her any sooner".

Kindness

Kindness was a beautiful brown old horse.
He was considerate and generous.

One day Kindness heard that there was going to be a race
between the hare and the tortoise.

Kindness loved to run. So he got himself registered for the race.

On the day of the race, the over confident hare felt that he would win without a doubt. So, the race began.

The Hare mocked the tortoise while passing her saying "oh my slow poach...you are never going to make it to the finish line. Na, na, na, na, nah". The Tortoise felt sad. But she chose to keep going.

Suddenly she looked around to find that Kindness the horse was also in the race. Kindness had passed them both swiftly in a few minutes and was in the lead.

She was surprised yet happy as she felt that someone would now overtake the Hare's over confidence.

But, alas! The Hare tripped into a thorn on the path. He screamed for help as he fell down. Kindness slowed down.

The Tortoise thought it was her chance to win so she kept running speedily. While passing the Tortoise on the way back, Kindness said to her "Hey I know the Hare was over confident. But now he is hurt and needs our help. A little kindness will be of good use".

The Tortoise thought for a minute and quickly realised that helping a friend with kindness was far more important than winning a race.

She slowed down and went along with Kindness to help the Hare get up. Together they gave him first aid.

The Hare was very grateful and also learnt that sometimes winning is not everything!

Honesty

Honesty was a good little boy in school. He was charming and intelligent too. Brody and Honesty were good friends.

Each of them wanted to be the teacher's favorite. So sometimes they argued about silly things.

One day Miss Emily was teaching the class when she heard the loud sound of a whistle. She turned around and looked at everyone in suspicion.

Brody accused Honesty of making that weird noise by saying "Ma'am, it was Honesty, I'm sure it was him, it was him!" Immediately Honesty replied saying "No ma'am, he's lying! I don't even have a whistle."

But Brody continued "ma'am he's only pretending. I saw him use a whistle right now. It's in his bag I'm telling you". Honesty retorted "No, no, ma'am. There is nothing of the sort. He's just ly...." and then Honesty took a minute to breathe.

Honesty looked again at Brody and said firmly
"Do not say lies Brody, it is not a good virtue!"
The school bell rang. Ma'am told the boys to pack up and
dismissed the class.

The next day while Brody was playing football, Stuart tripped him by running right into him. Brody called out saying it was a foul. But Stuart denied pushing him.

Finally the matter was settled that it was a foul. Stuart was ashamed of his lie and agreed that he did lie in order to win. Brody understood that he had done wrong to Honesty. He went to Miss Emily and said "Ma'am, please forgive me as I said a lie that day. Honesty did not have a whistle. I was just trying to be the best in front of you"

Miss Emily hugged Brody and said "I'm glad you realised your mistake. Now go and apologize to Honesty as well"

Then Brody approached Honesty and said "Sorry Honesty, I did lie after all. But now I do realize it is a bad virtue." He hugged Honesty and they reconciled immediately.

Respect

Respect was a lovely little old elf. He lived alone in a small cottage way up on a hill top. He was very hardworking and respectful.

Maryanne and Gizelle were two sisters. Maryanne was 15 while Gizelle was only 7 years old. Every evening all the children along with the old elf would come to Maryanne and Gizelle's garden to play.

One day while playing, Gizelle slipped accidentally and hurt her ankle. She looked up at Maryanne asking "Can you please get me some water Maryanne?"

But Maryanne refused saying "Go get it for yourself!" and walked away. Gizelle felt hurt but got up slowly and went inside the house limping.

Respect called Maryanne aside and said "Why did you do that? Gizelle only asked for water because she was hurt and couldn't walk." Maryanne responded "She is way younger than me and needs to respect me. I should not be getting up to fetch her water or anything."

Respect explained to Maryanne "Respecting each other has no age barrier. If you learn to give respect, you will also get some back." Maryanne again ignored the wise old elf and walked away.

A few days passed by and again the kids were playing in the garden.
This time Maryanne stumbled upon a rock and hurt her knee.

She looked around for help but all the children walked away.
Maryanne remembered that she had done the same to Gizelle.

She immediately realised her mistake and agreed that she did not act or treat Gizelle with all fairness.

She also realised the words of Respect and said to him "Thank you for helping me learn that everyone deserves respect as it has no barriers."

Love

Love was a pretty girl. Her favourite people were her family.
She had one elder brother named Ryan.
Love was adored by everyone except Ryan. He was a tad bit jealous
because she was quite favored being the baby of the family.

One day Love was crying as she wanted the same chocolate that Ryan had. Mommy asked Ryan to give it to Love saying "My darling, let her have it. She is only a baby."

Ryan gave it away unwillingly and sat sulking in the corner of the room.

His mother said "Don't be upset. She is your sister after all and if you love her, you must allow her to be happy."

Ryan responded "No, I don't love her! I don't want her to be happy. I'll only love her if she gives me that chocolate back!"

Mommy explained to Ryan gently "My son, love is unconditional and should not be based on actions and reactions." Ryan did not understand what his mother had said.

A few days later Love brought a similar chocolate home from a birth-day celebration in school. She ran straight to Ryan and said "You can have my chocolate today Ryuu. I saved it for you."

Ryan's eyes began to sparkle with joy and amazement as he wondered how selflessly his sister had acted not based upon anything.

He went to his mother and said "I'm sorry mama, I now understand what unconditional love is. I see it in the eyes of Love and I promise to be the same with her forever."

www.ingramcontent.com/pod-product-compliance
Lightning Source LLC
Chambersburg PA
CBHW041646110726

48005CB00003B/724